A SMALL HOUSE IN THE SUN

THE SHORT HOUSE, (1717). *Newbury, Mass.*

A SMALL HOUSE IN THE SUN

THE VISAGE OF
RURAL NEW ENGLAND

Photographs and Comment
by
SAMUEL CHAMBERLAIN

HASTINGS HOUSE   NEW YORK CITY

VILLAGE   *Marblehead, Mass.*

Copyright 1936, by
SAMUEL CHAMBERLAIN.

PRINTED IN THE UNITED STATES OF AMERICA.

COUNTRYSIDE   *Thomaston, Maine*

CONTENTS

	Page
FOREWORD	7
PART ONE—THE SETTING	9
The Village	9
The Rural Scene	21
The Seacoast	29
PART TWO—THE HOUSE	37
The Gambrel Roofed House	39
The Pitch Roofed House	51
The Small Two-Story House	65
Varied Examples	77
Old Doorways	87
CONCLUSION	95

SEACOAST *Gloucester, Mass.*

To the best of the author's knowledge, none of the houses illustrated is contemporary.

Stonington, Conn.

FOREWORD

There is one classic portrait of rural New England. It is composed of a field, a stone wall, and an old white house in the shade of two enormous trees. A great many things are expressed by such a simple landscape. It reflects the energy, courage and fortitude of the early New Englander. It hints at his family tradition, which dates back to the wedding day of his distant ancestors, when those two trees were planted symbolically before the front door. It speaks strongly of his ability to build substantially and in good taste.

Topsham, Maine

The soul and sinew of New England are tied up in its old houses. Some of them are stately mansions on the village green. Some are spacious farmhouses or rambling old inns. But greatest in number are the small houses, the homes of the average citizens of yesterday, today and, unless urbanism swallows us completely, for some time to come.

It is the small house of New England, and its setting in village, farm and seacoast, which furnish the theme of these photographs.

Thomaston, Maine

PART ONE—THE SETTING

THE VILLAGE

An old New England village stretches its sunny silhouette against a girdle of trees. It may lie on a hillside such as this, or in a valley, or on the riverbank or the seacoast. It may have built up around a small factory, or a boarding school or a fleet of fishing boats. Perhaps it lives on its carefully nourished tobacco fields or its Summer tourists.

Whatever its occupation may be, its heart beat is pretty sure to be found in the small, self-respecting white house which occupies the greater part of its tree lined streets, and which shelters the average New England family.

Community life calls for more than homes, however. There are other buildings which form a vital, almost compulsory part of the village scene. Let us look at them first, to visualize the surroundings in which the small house has developed. A slightly flattering composite would show . . .

The Brick Church

Lancaster, Mass.
Charles Bulfinch, Architect.

The Wooden Church

Longmeadow, Mass.

11

The Library

Farmington, Conn.

The General Store

South Sudbury, Mass.

The Post Office   Central Village, Mass.

The Town Hall

South Glastonbury, Conn.
(Recently Destroyed)

Main Street...

SPRING — Marblehead, Mass.

SUMMER — Exeter, N. H.

Main Street . . .

AUTUMN   Medford, Mass.

WINTER   Concord, Mass.

The Mansion　　　　　　　　　　　　　　　　　　　　　　　Portsmouth, N.H.

The Green　　　　　　　　　　　　　　　　　　　　　　　　Wenham, Mass

The Schoolhouse	Goshen, Conn.

The Old Inn	Golden Ball Tavern, (1753), Weston, Mass.

The Stately Avenue

WHITE CLAPBOARDS... *Exeter, N. H.*

AND WEATHERED ONES. *Old Deerfield, Mass.*

Stow, Mass.

THE RURAL SCENE

The small house is an integral part of the New England landscape. It brightens the country road. It figures in most farm groups, and often it *is* the farm. A glance at the rural backdrop may be informative . . .

The Landscape

MORNING   *Greenfield Hill, Conn.*

NOON   *South Sudbury, Mass.*

The Landscape

AFTERNOON *Niantic, Conn.*

SUNSET *Thomaston, Maine.*

The Farm

SPRING   *Lincoln, R. I.*

SUMMER   *Niantic, Conn.*

The Farm

AUTUMN — *Lincoln, Mass.*

WINTER — *Newton Upper Falls, Mass.*

The Mill Pond   *Fairfield, Conn*

The Barn

NEAR THE SEA... *Barnstable, Mass.*

AND INLAND *South Berwick, Maine*

The Cider Mill — Fairfield, Conn.

The Covered Bridge — Woodstock, Vermont

South Dartmouth, Mass.

THE SEACOAST

The proximity of the sea is often reflected in New England cottages. And many a ship's carpenter has left behind samples of his craftsmanship on the shore.

Seascape

DAWN — South Dartmouth, Mass.

MORNING — Rockport, Mass.

Seascape

AFTERNOON *Stonington, Conn.*

TWILIGHT *Noank, Conn.*

The Lighthouse   Stonington, Conn.

The Dunes   Provincetown, Mass.

The Windmill   Eastham, Mass.

The Docks   Rockport, Mass.

The Derelict

Wiscasset, Maine

The Bowsprits — Rockland, Maine

The Harbor — Boothbay Harbor, Maine

The Inlet

Old Lyme, Conn.

Mystic, Conn.

PART TWO—THE HOUSE

Against such a background, along these village streets, against these trees, the modest form of the old New England house has risen. A hardy and courageous people have built it compactly and well, to withstand the rigorous Winter. It is amazingly well suited to its surroundings, so much so, in fact, that close to three centuries have failed to develop a more suitable form. The gambrel, the pitch roof and the "salt box" are being built today, as they were in the time of Miles Standish.

Nine out of ten small New England houses are trim, substantial and practical, possessed of agreeable lines, but of no absorbing interest. But the tenth house is apt to be exceptional. Its window spacing is provocative, or its roof line is out of the ordinary, or its detail bears close study. It is likely to be rich in ideas for the contemporary home builder, even though these ideas came over from England but shortly after the Mayflower.

Three distinct types of small house assert themselves: the gambrel roofed house, the pitch roofed house and the small two-story dwelling which developed from the historic "salt box". Besides these, there are numerous others which refuse to be pigeon-holed.

One house out of ten should be interesting, architecturally and historically. Witness, for example, the development of the gambrel roofed type . . .

South Sudbury, Mass.

Harlow House (1677), Plymouth, Mass.

THE GAMBREL ROOFED HOUSE

A flawless and amazingly well preserved example left by the early Pilgrims.

Harlow House (1677), *Plymouth, Mass.*

There is plenty of precedent for the gambrel roof in America. This one was built with timbers brought from England less than twenty years after the Pilgrims landed!

Fairbanks House (1636), *Dedham, Mass.*

The pure Cape Cod type, without the suspicion of a
dormer. The unsymmetrical window spacing is subtle.

Chatham, Mass.

The son of Miles Standish built this gambrelled
homestead in 1666, within sight of Plymouth Harbor.

Duxbury, Mass.

The early Connecticut version is symmetrical and dormerless. The ridiculous chimney is a replacement.

South Windsor, Conn.

Two restrained dormers make their appearance on this weathered veteran.

Old Deerfield, Mass.

Another timid dormer, and a charming disregard of symmetry.

Old Tarr Homestead, Rockport, Mass.

The roof line, the doorway and the room arrangement are abruptly changed.

Guilford, Conn.

A gambrel fits well in any landscape. *Westport, Mass.*

A gambrel roof can turn a corner. *Glastonbury, Conn.*

Three dormers make their appearance. *South Sudbury, Mass.*

A brick example with flat dormers *Farmington, Conn.*

Two dormers and a noble chimney. The house must have looked much the same in Revolutionary times.

Watertown, Mass.

An ingenious combination of a gambrel and a salt-box roof.

Kingston, Conn.

Rarely is this end of a gambrel roofed cottage used as a street facade.

Cheshire, Conn.

A house more snugly settled in the ground would be hard to find.

Stonington, Conn.

The porch is a natural outgrowth on a gambrel roofed house...

Woodbury, Conn.

Greenfield Hill,

Ridgefield, Conn.

Essex, Conn.

Dorchester, Mass.

Hingham, Mass.

The gambrel roof climbs higher, and an entranceway appears.

Hingham, Mass.

Woodstock, Vermont

Eastham, Mass.

THE PITCH ROOFED HOUSE

The pitch roofed cottage flourishes abundantly on Cape Cod. That rather vague term, "Cape Cod House" usually refers to this simple type.

East Dennis, Mass.

Weathered shingles, white painted trim, a whitewashed chimney and a clear blue sky — these are the essence of Cape Cod.

Sandwich, Mass.

A group of minor farm buildings often strings out behind the house.

Duxbury, Mass.

An unsymmetrical but well balanced group.

South Dennis, Mass.

Warmth, dignity and repose are reflected in this symmetrical facade.

South Hingham, Mass.

The Connecticut valley farmer belongs in this prim, restrained little house.

Northford, Conn.

A sturdy old island house, possessed of fine proportions.   *Vinalhaven, Maine*

One senses in this sober dwelling the rigorous Winter climate of a Cape Ann fishing port.   *Rockport, Mass.*

A later Cape Cod type, undistinguished variations of which are found by the thousands.

South Dennis, Mass.

A street level floor has been neatly achieved.

Mystic, Conn.

Extreme simplicity, touched
off by a rather fine doorway.

Hampton, Conn.

Getting down to bare essentials.

Stow, Mass.

The farm buildings are attached to the house, a fact which the chore boy appreciates in Winter time!

Wiscasset, Maine

A picturesque interlocking of parts. The roof has a subtle bow.

Sandwich, Mass.

Morning shadows in Maine.

Wiscasset, Maine

This house can sprout dormers, two porches and four chimneys and still remain small and restful.

Greenfield Hill, Conn.

Second-story windows creep timidly into the facade . . .

Brookfield Center, Conn.

Wilton, Conn.

as do dormer windows.

Lexington, Mass.

Hingham, Mass

Wings sprout on many a pitch roofed house . . . .

South Hingham.

South Hingham

Milton, Mass.

and the appendages take on many forms.

Damariscotta, Maine

Wiscasset, Maine

Southbury, Conn.

A simple, pitch-roofed house can expand in many directions.

Dedham, Mass.

Marion, Mass.

Parson Capen House, (1683), Topsfield, Mass.

THE SMALL TWO-STORY HOUSE

A long sloping rear roof, an overhanging second story and a noble chimney—these were essentials in the early two-story houses of New England.

Ipswich, Mass.

A fine example of the "salt-box," and the birthplace of a President.

John Quincy Adams Birthplace, (1716), Quincy, Mass.

Serene after centuries.

Gloucester, Mass.

A small and most unusual variation of the "salt-box" theme.

Windsor, Conn.

Among the earliest and noblest in New England.

Balch House, (circa 1638), Beverly, Mass.

One imagines a sea captain living in this little house. The chimneys are unique.

Portsmouth, N.H.

A bit down at the heel, but filled with interest, due to its diminutive scale and its amusing overhang.

West Hartford, Conn.

A perfect bit of atmosphere to survive from the days of witchcraft!

Ipswich, Mass.

Four seasons of the small two-story house...

SPRING *Northford, Conn.*

SUMMER *Andover, Mass.*

AUTUMN

Dedham, Mass.

WINTER

Farmington, Conn.

New England knows no facade better than this, the smiling visage of the classic-inspired house.

Washington, Conn.

A "salt-box" of exquisite proportion. *Griswold House, (1750), Guilford, Conn.*

Here the lines are less flowing. *Captain Isaac Tucker House, (1789), Milton, Mass.*

A small New England house contrives many window spacings...

East Windsor, Co

Ipswich, Mass.

South Hingham,

and many a roof line.

Concord, Mass.

Lexington, Mass.

Lincoln, Mass.

Frequently found in Maine is the facade with four windows upstairs and down. The doorway is relegated to the side.

Topsham, Maine

Westport, Conn.

Woodstock, Vermont

VARIED EXAMPLES

In lower Connecticut an individual, low-roofed type of small house has taken root.

Silvermine, Conn.

The upper-story barely provides head room. In Summertime this blossoms into an antique shop.

Wilton, Conn.

The "Three Bears Inn" is faced with wide, whitewashed timbers. *Westport, Conn.*

The influence of the "saltbox" still seems to be felt. *Wilton, Conn.*

As New England as anything can be. *Westport, Mass.*

A restored relic of Colonial days.
Coach house of the Wayside Inn. *South Sudbury, Mass.*

Old law offices have a home-like quality.

Westminster, Vermont

This served as the law offices of Artemus Ward, Jr., and Isaac Fiske. Built 1785.

Weston, Mass.

A fisherman's house is apt to be rich in atmosphere . . .

Marblehead, Mass.

Ogunquit, Maine

silvery shingles and external trappings.

Rockport, Mass.

Rockport, Mass.

THE HILLSIDE WELL

Vernon, Conn.

e Gothic Touch,
(1827),
okline, Mass.

Barn Attached,
swick, Maine

he Twins,
ingham, Mass.

Two unsymmetrical cottages in balance.   *Farmington, Conn.*

Stoneham, Mass.

Exeter, N. H.

OLD DOORWAYS

Marblehead, Mass.

Exeter, N.H.

Salem, Mass.

Straitsville, Conn.

New Haven, Conn.

Wiscasset, Maine

Northford, Conn.

Slatersville, R. I.

Kennebunkport, Maine

Woodstock, Vermont

Bristol, R. I.

Portsmouth, N. H.

Old Deerfield, Mass.

Smithfield, R. I.

Newbury, Mass.

Portsmouth, N. H.

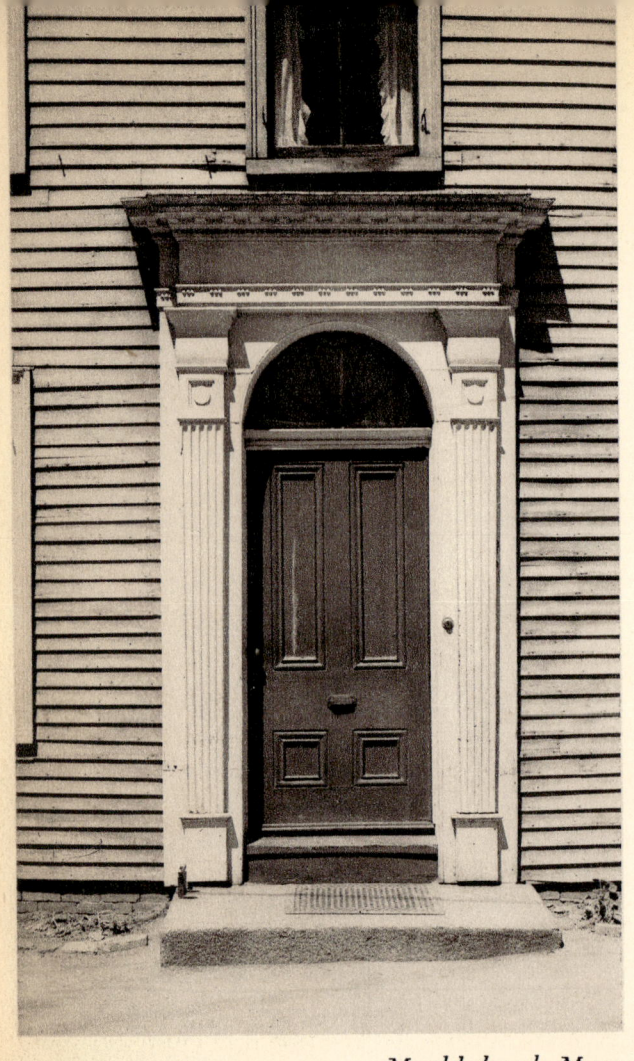

Marblehead, Mass.

Old Deerfield, Mass.

Marblehead, Mass.

Exeter, N. H.

Hadley, Mass.

South Windsor, Conn.

Gloucester, Mass.

Stockbridge, Mass.

Medford, Mass.

Newburyport, Mass.

Saugus, Mass.

Ashton, R. I.

Ogden House, Fairfield, Conn.

CONCLUSION

This book has dealt with smiling externals. Behind these doorways, these clapboards and shingled sides, there lies a more intimate symbol of early New England, the hearth.

A picture quite as appealing as the small house in the sun, and even closer to the heart of the New Englander, can be woven around the rural hearthside.

But that is another story, and a fascinating one!

THE END.

Vinalhaven, Maine

728 C44
Chamberlain, Samuel, 1895-
A small house in the sun;
the visage of rural New
England;

DISCARDED

DATE DUE			
MAR 24 2007			
DEC 13 2005			
JUL 20 2007			